Recline In My Soul

Jeweled words kissing the heart to heaven

Dedicated to supporting
the birth of the Mystic Lover
into humanity

JAYEM

Recline In My Soul

Second Edition

www.wayofmastery.com

Published by:
Heartfelt Publishing PMA
PO Box 204, Ubud 80571
admin@wayofmastery.com

ISBN: 978-602-98911-7-1

© 2002 Jayem

Publication or reproduction of this work, in whole or in part, by any means whatsoever, without the written permission of the author is prohibited.

Contents

Author's Introduction vii

POEMS

The Call: Tilling the Soil of the Soul

Not My Own 3
Here 4
While Sleeping 5
Homecoming Dance 6
Wait 7
Ode to Hana 8
Order Up 10
Like Melting Snow 11
Jasmine Moonlight 12

Revelations: Comments from a Choiceless Surrender

Beach Walk 17
Showering Tears 18
Shimmering One 19
Crimson Embrace 20
Taking Pause 21
Memory of a Dream 22
Prey 23
The Fool 24

In The Key of Love: Glimpses of the Real World

A Useless Attempt 27
Be Watchful 28
This Sweet Love 29
Springtime 30
The Grace-filled Face 31
Touch of Grace 32
It's the Real Thing 33
Pinnacle 34
The Strange Land 35

The Whisper 36
No Doors, Only the Dark 37
The Matchstick 38

Sweet Beloved: The Transformation of Romantic Love

Place Mat 41
Shhhhh..42
Pilgrimage 43
Who Can Say? 44
Something Greater 45
Songbirds...46
There Must Be More 47
What a State...48
Crumbling..49
Alas 50
Love is the Fire..52
Unheard Laughter 53
Quick! 54
The Field 55
Leaf-Covered Lane 56
Consort 57
Clay House..58
Peek-a-Boo 59
Carried Away..60
Upside Down 61
Two Hearts..62
Our Journey 63
The Best of Sex..64

Soul: All We Need to Remember

The Reed Flute..67
Second Birth 68
Oops! 70

The Friend: Grace Takes a Shape to Which We May Respond

The Friend...73
A Question for the Avatar..74
The High Mountain..75
Oh, Friend! 76

Gifts of Sophia: Fruits from Well Planted Seeds

A Piece of Coal 81
The Presence That Doesn't 82
Karma to Dharma 83
Like A Jewel 84
The Joke is on Me 85
Mask-Maker 86
The One Request 88
The Gambler 89
Mystic Fool 90
This Old House 92
Mocking the Beloved 93
May Lightening Strike 94
Fruit on the Tree 95
Disappearing 96
No One Here 97
Sleeping Stones 98
The Caravan 100
There is a Place 102
Become That Fire 103
In G-d's Defense 104
Where Goodness Shines 106
Become Wise 107
Purest Gold 108
Intoxicating Embrace 109
The Fisherman 110
Performance Anxiety 111
Silver Palms 112
I See You 113
The Tortoise and the Hare 114
Which Floor? 115
Who Arrives? 116

About the Author 119

Author's Introduction

I am a child of the sixties. I remember the summer of 1967 when—as a high school sophomore—I drove with a friend from Washington State to San Francisco. The Haight-Ashbury district, to be exact. There was a certain something wafting through the air there, and I speak of no material substance!

1970 found me in the jungles of Vietnam where—as company radioman—I occasionally helped call in devastating air strikes, along with living miraculously through the usual firefights and helicopter extractions.

If Haight-Ashbury however crudely revealed the possibility of a new kind of consciousness, Vietnam began my personal odyssey to it, for there I felt the impact of forces not my own that, on more than one occasion, saved my life. One day, while lifting my head from the monotonous tedium of digging yet another foxhole to watch the sunset, I suddenly felt stretched to infinity; embracing all things, pervading all things, free of all things. It would be pitch dark before I found myself again an eighteen-year-old soldier, holding a shovel.

"God, if there is such a thing, I must know what that was, and, and what *this*, this world, is all about!" I said it more with anger than hope, and heard no reply in the deep jungle darkness.

Once I arrived back home, I 'just happened' to stumble upon yoga and meditation, and 'just happened' to take a philosophy class from a man who would be my first mentor, or *guru*. He could wipe dust from his teak desk with a presence and love that was palpable, not to mention appearing physically in two different places! A true yogi, in disguise as a college professor.

I steeped myself in yoga and meditation, grew into samadhi and certain *siddhi* (paranormal powers), and studied psychology, philosophy, and religion. It would take many steps on the Path before I realized God had not only heard my prayer that night in Vietnam, but had immediately set about to answer it in the only way that could work, and that is *never our own*. But from the moment all of one's being is unified in the desire for God, That One embraces the soul, fashions it for the journey, and carries it in its perfect currents, home, to Itself.

Awakening is, in the end, a strange alchemical mixture of one's desire and constant confession of ignorance, and the Grace Stream the Divine breathes in our direction.

These poems are a collection of words which often flowed through my fingertips to my keyboard as I would sit at my desk in meditation late in the evenings, lost in the contemplation of God, or wondering into the depth of my life's events. They were discovered when I decided to clean out my computer's hard drive, scattered willy-nilly in this file or that!

It became clear reading through them that they naturally fall into stages of the process of awakening. First, **The Call** offers words literally from a Voice not my own. Contrary to the general view of empirical psychology prevalent in our world, the evolution of consciousness *does* reveal and cultivate a connection, as it were, with a Spirit beyond our own, a Spirit that plugs one intimately and directly into the Source, the Suchness, the Heart of the Creator. It is not the 'frontal personality,' the egoic self, which can know this transcendent illumination, much less discover how to operate from it in life.

Next, in **Revelations**, I offer suggestions on how we may look upon this great seat of our Existence, and begin to shape our orientation to Life along the lines of a loving relationship willingly served.

And what can the spiritual journey do if not quicken the soul with an ever-deepening experience of what Love is, and is for? **In the Key of Love** offers a few guideposts—and challenges—as the soul's basic orientation to this heart of Divine Mystery is re-made, and not by itself.

Sweet Beloved offers poems from my own relationship with a wonderful divine lover, and reveals how even the most basic of human desires is transformed by the caress of the Divine, until one can no longer tell where the beloved one ends and the Beloved Divine begins. And even if the beloved one should leave, the Beloved Divine is not lost.

> *Freed from the tyranny of the fear of loss,*
> *love fulfills the soul.*

Next are a few verses on ***Soul: All We Need to Remember*** since, well, this *is* all we need remember.

The Friend includes a few selected writings honoring a simple fact: no one awakens even a little without the help of others. God is speaking through them: the right message at the right time.

For me, the Friend who comes as final *Guru* first appeared before me in a field of shimmering light in 1987. It was Jeshua (Y'shua, Jesus). Whoever comes to serve us, the Friend deeply imprints the soil of the soul with seeds from God's storehouse, destined to grow much good fruit (while shattering the grip of egoic identity).

Finally, in ***Gifts of Sophia***, I offer 'wisdom-bytes' as a sharing of ideas exactly as I received them, as though taking down dictation hurriedly to catch up with what was already penetrating my soul. *Sophia* is the feminine Greek word for wisdom, suggesting humans have always intuited that the Divine must finally be approached in surrender and a mind softened from habits of opinions, judgments, and defenses. Its translation eventually becomes what we know today as the 'Holy Spirit.'

These words are not meant to be **read** but, rather, to be **digested** in a kind of contemplative consideration, more in feeling and absorbing them—the very spirit of Sophia, I would suggest. They reveal certain important insights into the universal template through which each soul is obliged to evolve. With this approach, your precious time with them will bear good fruit, as they have for so many others.

. . . . .

The Divine Mystery reveals itself in three essential ways, and a brief description here will enhance your reading experience.

First, I write 'God' as 'G-d' in honor of the Jewish wisdom that the Divine is utterly unknowable in any final sense. Remembering this liberates us from arrogance, and frees us to be humbly present in, and *for*, each moment.

As impersonal and universal energy, G-d is the Shimmering One, whose radiance is everywhere obvious when mystical sight is opened.

As the Creator, it becomes clear we are the created, yet the idea of a 'jealous, wrathful God' dissolves into the notion of G-d as the *Beloved One*, affectionately calling us out into an ever-deepening, ever-expanding, and—at times—ever self-shattering relationship. Through the alchemy of transformation, the soul discovers itself to be G-d's very play. G-d *does not judge* Creation. G-d *grows* its capacity to know and extend the *Good*, the *Holy*, and the *Beautiful*.

Briefly, the 'Imposter' is my term for the ego/false self, for any awakening mystic knows that even the 'healthy and well-adjusted self,' prized as the height of evolution in empirical psychology and equally so in popular religion (it is the self we hope God will save), is no more than a pesky gnat from the vantage point of transpersonal awareness.

G-d is the Gardener, we only the soil. We cannot live Life. We can only finally consent to allowing Life to live us, *for* Itself. This is how the heart is kissed into Heaven.

Streams of Joy,
Jayem
Maui, Hawaii, May, 2002

For Melea

Whose love and friendship have grown my soul
and who inspired me to gather these words together
as a gift for fellow sojourners.

Now…

Abide quietly with me.
Allow your breath to find its natural and unhurried way;
feel it streaming in and deep into your belly.
Let the exhale carry away all tension, feeling
the silence – there – at the end of the outbreath.

Enjoy the breath for a few minutes
as the mind settles down,
and attention turns inward to the heart.

Trust…

Remember you are loved
and safe in the arms of G-d,
however you may conceive of That One.

Pray…

"Allow me to receive through these words
the jewels of healing wisdom that only You
would feed my soul at this time.
I rest in You, as I rest into my very Self.
Thank you for my life.
Thank you, thank you, thank you."

Reside in the breath again as though it were
the 'chair' in which you sit.

Now,
turn the page,
and 'recline in my soul'…

The Call

Tilling the Soil of the Soul

Not My Own

A startling Voice not my own
echoed from everywhere:

> **"Listen...**
> Can you hear My call?
>
> There!
> Just beneath the conflict of illusions
> churning in your mind am I calling...
>
> Come,
> sweet and wondrous one, come!
> Arise from your slumber and embrace
> all I would give you:
> the kiss of a friend who accepts all of you,
> the grace that dissolves all karma,
> the peace that showers down upon you unearned.
>
> Your soul is My breath.
> You carry Me throughout unending worlds.
>
> Still the noise 'round your heart and behold:
> I am already there, deep inside,
> near as I can be to My most precious creation:
> You!
>
> This Now can be the moment
> you have always secretly longed for,
> waiting,
> waiting on your welcome of Me.
>
> Listen...
>
> Can you hear My call?"

Here

"Look at me!" cried my Beloved.

"Where are you?" I asked.

"Here!" came the reply, "Here!"

"Where is 'here?' I don't see you!" I shouted.

" 'Here'
is deeper than your coveted thoughts,
prior to your very breath
and forever unreachable
by the avenues of your theologies
and spiritual strategies.

The only way to arrive 'Here'
is to abandon the self in devotion to Love."

While Sleeping

I fell asleep one night listening to the breezes
dance with the branches of the palm tree
outside my window.

Then my Beloved bent low to whisper in my ear, saying:

> *"The wise do nothing,*
> *knowing that without Me*
> *only illusions can arise from the soil of their minds.*
>
> *They dedicate themselves ceaselessly*
> *to refining their ability to hear only My voice*
> *moment to moment, breath to breath.*
>
> *For them do I translate time into eternity,*
> *reclining their souls in the place*
> *I alone can prepare for them,*
> *replacing the death of self-dreams*
> *with Life.*
>
> *The world in all its concerns fades from them,*
> *and they are melted into ongoing, flowing Mystery,*
> *knowing only that Something Else lives through them.*
>
> *They live not as seekers,*
> *choosing to leap 'cross the abyss of Trust*
> *and delight in making this decision to be found,*
> *a decision that can be made*
> *even while listening to the wind*
> *dance through this palm tree!"*

I awoke with a start,
the choice between life or death
in the palm of my hand.

Homecoming Dance

> *"Come!*
> *Surrender the world you have made*
> *and learn to dance in the fire of My Fire!"*

thundered the Beloved.

> *"For behold!*
> *That one who flees the Imposter's dreams*
> *and learns to dance in the fire of my Fire,*
> *that one*
> *shall I lift ever higher and higher*
> *until they are so consumed in Me*
> *that only I pour out to the world*
> *through mind, gesture, and vision.*
>
> *What greater good could you achieve*
> *than to melt the resistance to Me*
> *crusting away the inner edges of your very veins,*
> *and shaping your thoughts into arrows of fear?*
>
> *Give Me away thoroughly, and you have Me.*
>
> *Have Me not, and have nothing."*

Quick! I hear the music starting.
Let's buy tickets to this Firewalk for everyone!

Wait

"Wait!
Do not be so quick
to believe the body's eyes;
I have not gone.

Turn your gaze inward
and feel your heart, and deeper still,
plunging, surrendering,
into the Heart of your beating heart
where only eternity can survive;
I am here.

Breathe in My caress
as My delight pulses through the lips of your soul
when — turned from all creations —
they join with Mine,
here,
in this sublime and sacred place
not even the body can reach to.

Wait here, with Me.
It is enough; it is all.
Let every doing through you become Mine.

Wait here, with Me."

Ode to Hana

My Beloved never fails to seduce me here,
away from movies this useless mind seems to make
when I have forgotten Her, like some
poor beggar who thinks a hundred dollar bill
is too heavy to carry, and so casts it away.

Gone,
the clatter of our world spinning too fast to see, to taste,
to dissolve into this delicious Beauty flowing from Mystery,
flowing through rainbow clouds and rushing waterfalls,
flowing through the songbird's sunrise call,
flowing through this streaming breath that pulls me into
the silent center.

Remembrance comes easily here, cradled in Eden,
where surely my Beloved
places Her heart for safekeeping.

Her sweet voice whispers:

> *"Dissolve, dissolve all yesterdays and the sea of your
> tomorrows in this sensuous presence of Me.*
>
> *I will caress you in My breezes, kiss you in My scents,
> and rock you to sleep in My velvet darkness.*
>
> *In dreams I will heal you
> and carry your soul to realms unimagined,
> for I am here – already closer to you than your very breath.*

*I am the Beauty
by which you behold what is beautiful.
I am the Good
by which you behold what is good.
I am the Holiness
by which you behold what is holy.*

*Come, my creation! Come!
Let me dissolve you like mist
before the rising sun."*

Order Up

"What would you suggest from the possibility menu today?"
I asked my Beloved.

The Shimmering One smiled,
happy that I took the time to ask.

> *"This day,*
> *let Me love you through*
> *all you see,*
> *all you taste,*
> *all you hear,*
> *and all that you smell.*
>
> *And give Me to all you meet*
> *through your kindness,*
> *aware that I am the secret house guest*
> *they carry with them*
> *wherever they go."*

What was I to do?
So much for the plans formulating
in my foaming and restless mind!

Surrendered now,
this cup of coffee, this wisp of breeze.

The doorbell.
Someone is in for a kiss upon their cheek!

Like Melting Snow

I asked my Beloved to show me the Way.
My Beloved whispered:

> *"Let me burn you up from the inside*
> *and you will change from solid ice to flowing water.*
>
> *Then I will know you are worthy of the Way."*

My soul replied,
"Show me to this fire and cast me in!"

Welcomed comes this ice-melting
of the Great Myth of "I."

Jasmine Moonlight

"Speak to me of your love, O Shimmering One!"

Came the voice as a thunderous whisper:

> *"My love is like the moonlight*
> *rippling over the ocean.*
> *Whether appearing as a broken dance*
> *or as a still reflection of its source,*
> *the light is the same.*
> *Make your mind like moonlight*
> *reflecting Me into the world,*
> *whether in repose or in storm.*
>
> *My love is like the roar of a lioness*
> *whose power flows from the body of certain strength,*
> *for the lion is master of her domain, fearing nothing.*
> *Make your mind like the lion revealing My power.*
>
> *My love is like the scent of night-blooming jasmine.*
> *Unseen in the dark of sleep,*
> *its caress is a blessing of safety and joy.*
> *Make your mind like jasmine,*
> *caressing the heart of everyone who but has*
> *a fleeting thought of you.*
>
> *My love is like the maiden*
> *who comes willingly to the marriage bed,*
> *longing only for utter surrender to her beloved.*
> *Make your mind like the maiden,*
> *and I alone your Beloved.*

*My love is like the deep quiet of night when
even the winds sleep fast.
Make your mind like the still night,
a womb embracing the world
and into which I can enter.*

*My love?
My love is like **you**
in those moments when you are surrendered in Me.
You know them:
wanting nothing but to enjoy the bliss of My presence
and to give Me away for the joy of doing so!
Make your mind emptied of your self
that I may spill out into the world through you."*

Revelations

Comments from a Choiceless Surrender

Beach Walk

Amazing!
An impulse of desire arises
and now I walk on warm sand at the ocean's edge.

The waves have come to be my symphony
as the sun drops its fiery red body into the sea.

Am I the guest of honor here?
Who is it that can give such things?
Surely,
it must be my Beloved.

Showering Tears

Oh, my!
This torrent of tears has caught hold of me,
here as I wash my bowl and cup.

My Beloved is cracking me open yet again,
revealing the sweet benevolence
of Her unyielding love for me!

Everything in my life
has Her healing touch upon it,
everything!

She leads me to the High Mountain to see:

My life is but the magnificent woven threads of Grace
given of Her freely.
She weaves the sacred carpet that flies me away
into the liquid gold
of her bosom.

My Beloved is unyielding in Her love for me,
always greater than my resistance
to the gift of even more of Her.

Shimmering One

You are the temple I rest in
the moment I remember that nothing else
holds any value at all.

For only Reality can have value.

This seems insane to those who insist
on valuing the valueless
and ignore the facts of their own experience:
worshipping the transitory is a sure recipe for suffering!

No other place would I wish to go
now that you have outwitted the Imposter,
seducing it to its own doom.

There is nothing to compare,
not riches nor fame nor any worldly thing,
for a moment's awareness of You
is a taste sweet above honey.

May this mind contain only
the constant awareness of You.

Crimson Embrace

Here with this haunting stringed music
the crimson embrace of the sun's last shout of day
carries me away,
away far beyond,
not outward, but in.

In and deeper still,
this Imposter dissolving more quickly
than the clouds
into the dark forgetting of night.

The body whispers the truth, though:
this sad longing for the touch of my Beloved
to penetrate me more deeply.
But even more:
to somehow shower this world of dreamers
with the grace of That Shimmering One,
stirring them to stop settling
for the crumbs the Imposter accepts!

Sweet Beloved, devour us
and make us Yours.

Taking Pause

Beloved, have I paused to love only You today?

Not my dreams nor myopic ideas,
nor my past creations,
nor present things.

Not love of flower or sea or sunrise,
but You, only You!

You pour out Your light upon me without ceasing.
Your delight in giving Yourself to my soul never wavers.

Oh, where am I?
Once I thought I knew:
here in this obvious and ordinary world,
one fish in the sea.

But now I am held in weightless safety,
each stepping stone set before me
before I even know the step will be taken.

Falling into Your abyss
I am caught in soft certainty,
placed by You where You would have me be
that I might grow ever more deeply
into this perfect love of You!

For You have created me only to praise You,
and more:

You set me free
so that I may learn to choose You,
the only good fruit in an orchard of illusions.

Memory of a Dream

Alas,
I have not done well.

I spent years devoted to the hope
of finding G-d.

But now that the Beloved has burnt up the Imposter
I can't remember myself long enough to say:
"I did it!"

When I am wrapped in the beguiling limbs of my Beloved,
there is no "me" to be found.

When I can find a "me"
I am like a sad puppy waiting for the Master to return.

By grace,
such moments grow fewer and fewer.

Prey

What mystery, this!
I write words flowing forth like a stream
emerging from a solid rock face,
and this miracle reveals:
I am not the writer at all!

Like you,
I am a witness of Mystery,
forever a student of the Beloved
who reveals Herself to fill the places She has carved out
from our fearful illusions.

Once, I sought G-d,
silly enough to think I could find Her
on the way I chose from my arrogance.

In the end, I relented,
and let myself be found.

The Shimmering One has devoured Her prey
and all that is left is this empty shell,
now filled and animated
by something closer to me than my own breath,
yet not my possession nor creation.

Love breathes me,
and I am Hers.

The Fool

The fool went to the oracle
who lives in the center of the heart's silence
and asked:

"When will I know Love?"

Came the reply, echoing within him, around him,
emanating as if through all creation:

> *"When you willingly dive into the Fire
> knowing the only result is death."*

The fool replied: "Okay."

In he dove, never to rise again.

Something Else took his place.
It looked curiously like him,
but if you got close you could tell.

There is a reason it is written:
"None can look on the face of G-d and live."
Would you think the Beloved would make an exception
for you?

Come close if you dare!
Die into the Something Else where once the fool existed.

In the Key of Love

Glimpses of the Real World

A Useless Attempt

Who can be penetrated
by the Beloved's sweet grace
while insisting
on how love should show up,
and what demands from it are acceptable?

Love,
like a wild stallion
running in fields of limitless freedom,
laughs at our expectations.

Only its unfathomable mystery
and inexhaustible well are
pure and absolute.

Be Watchful

Oh,
this mystery of Love!
She calls and we come to the edge and taste...
then sinking back we moan,
"I'm not ready."

Only those empty of themselves can stay with Her.
Only those as free with Her
as She is with them
can walk with Her
through infinite fields of creation,
beyond even
eternity's embrace of time.

All the while,
the Beloved waits in this very present moment
fully desiring to give Herself
to the soul of the world.

Be watchful!

Don't miss her caress,
and fail not to pass it on.

This Sweet Love

Entering the eternal mystery of Love is not a given.
It must be cultivated like a fine English garden,
cared for with great commitment,
and everything we have learned
about how things are done
will fail us
in this Garden.

For Love is another dimension altogether.

Will you choose to become the Capable Lover
in this very world,
while not being *of* this world?

Only in this way will Love reveal itself to you,
for Love comes only
to one who has shown the Beloved
they can handle her extraordinary Fires
that burn up the self and spew out its ashes.

As Love reveals itself
like sunlight through morning mists
to the one who has been shattered,
it is like the very sky opening to infinity,
like the phoenix flying beyond all worlds.

The mind is liberated into silence.
The heart is surrendered into peace.
The soul reclines in the Beloved,
going out no more from the holy of holies.

Springtime

A quiet unseen warmth
is the downfall of winter.

So, too,
does the simple choice for Love
melt away lifetimes of illusions.

Illusions are always, *always* about ourselves.
When deep,
they cast shadows that
seem to engulf the world.

More than this,
they make the world,
while the reality of the Shimmering One's presence
is undisturbed,
waiting like a gift at the base of a Christmas tree
to simply be received and opened
by a willing heart.

The Grace-filled Face

What cannot be brought to Love
and be dissolved in its radiance?

Can Love be loved
beyond the form of the beloved
and the desire of the lover?

Who can surrender to Love
and be without clinging,
which makes Love flee,
replaced by the Imposter who lives too well here?

If I say "I love you"
from the place within me that is not "me"
but Love,
then you are the one I set free.

And to be set free is what every soul secretly desires.

Should you remain with an open heart,
the grace-filled face of our Beloved
shines upon us and through us.

Let us give the gift we are secretly waiting to be given.

Touch of Grace

The purpose,
power,
and blessing of Love
is this:

only Love may transform us.

For it is Love
that birthed us
to make Itself manifest,
revealing its
Purpose.

It is Love
that opens our hearts
to the touch of Grace;
the life-kiss revealing its
Power.

And it is Love
whose movement through us
fulfills the soul,
revealing Love's blessing
upon us:

We are the messiah
sent in Love's Name to make Love known.

It's the Real Thing

Every genuine act of love is to be blessed,
by everyone.
Whenever Love is present between any two (or more)
it is undeniable.

How that love expresses is the Beloved made visible
and given as a blessing to this thirsty world,
for G-d is Love.

What is the proper orientation toward That One?

Worship and celebration and awe.

To do so is to taste the wine of real praise.

If we set limits on Love's expression
have we not judged the womb
of love's existence?

Love is genuine only when there is no need
for possession of the beloved,
for Love desires only to support, uplift, encourage,
and — above all —
allow complete freedom to the chosen beloved.

No flower grows where roots cannot dive deep,
nor branches extend outward
and upward.

Only by loving, so alone
do we awaken finally in the radical bliss
that we, too, are so loved;
we are free because we are *in*
Love.

Pinnacle

The pinnacle of the Beloved's mountain
every mystic climbs
is to finally not love at all.

"That is absurd!" the Imposter cries.

But the wise,
those who have sailed beyond the edge
of the world,
know they cannot choose love,
for it is Love that chooses them.

That is why
they are constantly emptying themselves
of personal agendas
and ridding themselves of the habit
of trying to store up and possess love
for a rainy day.
They surrender with every exhale
into the great abyss so feared
by most.

There,
beyond the edge of "I"
is the only power capable of truly revealing
the Beloved.

The Strange Land

This strange and familiar land
calls to me
across the veils of illusions
I once drew 'round myself
in expanding circles of amazing complexity.

In that land I once lived, with you.

If we dare answer the Beloved's call
will not the veils be shattered and dissolved
in the last tears of the Imposter?

Then the desert between this dream-world
and the Beloved's Garden
will be crossed in an ark made for us,
but not by us.

Not of wood or steel is our vessel made,
but Love.

And the land to which we are delivered
is the Real World,
shimmering beyond all boundaries,
here.

The Whisper

Crush life
from the sordid and stormy shadows
of frantic raw aching
and eat the sweet delicate light of love
flooding through you
like beautiful petals of pink roses,
dancing
in misty spring rains,
falling
down upon you like diamonds
in a moonless garden
of Stillness.

No Doors, Only the Dark

What have I gotten myself into?

Love has seduced me to return here,
to this darkness left far behind
and deep within,
but who can blame it?

For Love's only goal
is to transmute everything
which is **not** Love.

Turn about in the seat of your soul,
and give up your straining
for ever-greater
ascension.

Look willingly upon the shadows
yet remaining,
for if you find yourself as a body-mind
in the Beloved's house of many mansions
they are there seeking to devour you
like hungry ghosts.

Yet,
their embrace in Love
is the very act of union with G-d,
for it is That One who is the love
with which you will love the 'hell'
right out of you!

The Matchstick

Become destroyed in Love.

Then,
behold the Light of the Shimmering One
arising,
arising from deep inside
the place you were,
arising
like the radiant flame
from the death
of the matchstick.

Sweet Beloved

The Transformation of Romantic Love

Place Mat

What is this sweet place
where my life pours into yours
and yours into mine?

What is this convergence of consent,
this surrender
beyond the shells of the known,
revealing the Beloved calling through each of us
to the other?

Perhaps
we have not so much come to this place,
as it has come to us,
borne on the wings of Love,
asking of us only
the grace of a little willingness.

Shhhhh

What is this mystery that calls us here?

Who can bring such power to bear
that a quiet desire silently offered
in prayer
can be transformed into the joy
of your warm breath on my skin
as we rest from celebrating our thankfulness
for this grace that has joined us?

The Beloved does not answer
all prayer.
Only those She knows
will bring the praying closer
to Herself.

She is inside the desire of our desire.

Shhhhh...
Let's stop talking
and celebrate this miracle!

Pilgrimage

Oh, dear one!
I have forged the texts of a thousand wise men
and sat at the feet of countless masters
only to discover
that heaven is in the way
I trace this terrain
running from your shoulder to your breast
with my attentive tongue
in a state of utter, devotional prayer.

The Lord my G-d is a sensuous G-d,
for only such a One
could fashion this exquisite human skin
and wrap it so delicately 'round the purity and radiance
of such a soul
as yours.

Who Can Say?

This longing emerges
from some mysterious place
that is placeless
in the abyss of my heart.

All I asked for
was to know the shining center
of my Beloved.

After She had swept me up
from the weight of my illusions
and drenched me in her ecstatic white light,
she deposited me here,
and I found myself standing with you,
warmly smiling at me.

"Hmm," I muttered under my breath.
"My Beloved is playing sweet music on the harp
of my soul."

I ride the sacred notes
to the jeweled crescent of your
heart-temple.

Something Greater

The fire of the sun melts away
all that comes too close,
but is helpless before
a closed heart.

Something Greater is called for.

You greet me with sarong wrapped
about your waist,
but I see only this radiance streaming
from your smile
and drawing me into your eyes.

There is a great fire alive
within you,
fueled by your surrender to the Beloved.
Your smile its gesture,
your eyes the doorway to the One I Love.

What you are is Something Greater,
and my heart is thrown open even wider
to the delicious taste of
So Much Love.

Songbirds

Songbirds this early morning.
No need to rise.

The wine has been poured
and through the night we drank long and deep
together.

Now,
these songbirds with the dawn.
No need to rise.

We rest entwined
on the notes of this free chorus
with just enough quiet
to offer our prayers of thankfulness to the
Wine Maker.

Songbirds this early morning.
No need to rise.

There Must Be More

Look!
Love's waters emerge like a fountain
from some hidden unspeakable Mystery,
and already the lotuses blossom.

Look with me!

This fresh pond.

It emerges in the space of "we"
offered continually by the Beloved;
a gift of grace
made to adorn two "I's"
who want more of G-d so much
that they have been willing to worship
only at the altar of forgiveness.

This is a wine fine enough for any communion.

Drink up!

What a State

Look at me.
What a sad state I am in!

Reduced to a trust-it-all
where once I strove to be a know-it-all,
the eyes of my soul
are turned ceaselessly to the Beloved,
imploring Her to reveal to me
how this mere pauper
can hope to nurture the essence-being
of such a shining beauty
already intoxicated with the golden wine
streaming from the pitcher of the Friend
who restores all things.

At least I have learned enough
at the Beloved's feet
to begin each moment anew,
muttering prayers under my breath
that my life might carry some touch of Love
to the radiant beloved
set before me.

Crumbling

My soul
is opening like a flower
called by the warmth of the spring sun
flowing from your heart to mine.

You are the blessing of my Beloved
in whom your beauty was birthed
before time.

You are the blessing of my Beloved
in whom this call to a higher love echoes across
the feeble walls of my safe shell.

Crumbling,
I am here before you.

Naked, willing, and trusting,
wanting only that the Beloved love you
through me.

Surely,
only that One to whom you clearly belong
can offer you what you are worth.

Of myself,
I can only offer this temple as a sanctuary for you;
a place where you might recline
in the Soul of your soul.

Alas

I am certain I have found something wrong
with my Beloved's creation!

For surely Love decries separation
while these bodies offer it repeatedly.

You are there
and I am here,
here with this longing to translate
the light that comes from beyond the body
into a moment's gentle caress:
fingertips on cheek,
lips on the back of your neck.

Wait... a telegram from the Beloved is arriving...

Aha!
This time is not separation but
- as silence dances with notes to create a love song -
a temple to which our Beloved brings us
to savor the moments
of our bodies' closeness,
teaching us how to make love without them
as we linger in the sweetness
of the Real World
like butterflies in a meadow
of gratitude.

And so I celebrate this raw aching
so exquisitely dripping through
my being.

Separation is impossible
in the land between two hearts
where Love
has come to dwell.

Can you feel my breath
tracing the line
of your hip?

Love is the Fire

What am I to do?

When you are here
it is not sleep I am called to
but your arms,
and this deep alchemical fire we burn in,
there in the Inner Chamber.

When you are not here
I burn in this constant dance between this raw aching
and overwhelming gratitude
that causes me to laugh and cry
at the drop of a hat!

How am I to escape this all consuming heat?

I rush headlong into the Fire.

Unheard Laughter

How my Beloved has turned me inside-out!

All my striving and learning,
all the spiritual gymnastics and clever metaphysics
are reduced to less than
nothing.

Now,
I sit on this blanket
feeling your arms all about me,
hearing some passage sparkling in wisdom
you have drawn from an unnamed tome.

Jut this presence with you,
shimmering within and illuminating without,
reveals the Beloved to be resting
everywhere,
above board,
and obvious to anyone
whose eye has been made single.

Now,
this is real spiritual practice!

Quick!

How fleeting, this!

You are dissolving before my very eyes
along with this world I once naively took
as the real;
the day of last embrace speeds to me:
these bodies always fail.

Quick!
I must be quick, and certain,
letting no day be wasted in lack of
loving appreciation
and thankfulness to the Shimmering One
who holds us all.

Fleeting,
this embrace of flesh.

Yet,
embracing the world
as the Beloved
opens the soul to eternity.

Why settle for less than everything?

The Field

Something in the magical flow of this divine mystery
which has carried them to each other's shore
triggers the edge of fear resting in their closets,
tucked away in their cellars.

But that is what Love is good at, and good for.

Beyond the edges
is a field of lavender and jasmine
and the shade of the sandalwood tree.
Only Love can see the field,
while fear obscures it like some dreary winter fog.

Our Beloved whispers:

> *"Walk with Me a little further still, and know:
> it is but My Love that calls you past
> the limit of your worlds."*

Agreeing to do so,
the field appears all around them,
stretching far as the eye can see,
and, look!

There are no edges this love cannot dissolve!

And so they rest,
hidden in the grasses,
pouring golden wine into each other's cup
by which to toast their union!

Leaf-Covered Lane

The gate rests to the side opened for us,
but not by us.

Autumn leaves gladly fall from their homes
to give us softness and beauty upon which
to walk hand in hand
down this enchanting lane, attractive and unknown.

"Where will this path take us?"
I ask the Beloved with eyes closed.

Came the reply, singing its way to our ears
through the swirling and whirling of these brilliant,
colored leaves:

> *"The destination is already revealed in how,*
> *hands joined, you come to Me with each step,*
> *two 'I's' surrendered into 'we.'*
>
> *Who else could bring you here*
> *to meet through your eyes cleansed by My grace*
> *revealing not appearances*
> *but the essence of your very souls?*
>
> *Who with a breath could cast these leaves*
> *beneath your feet?*
>
> *Remember:*
> *These leaves and this lane are Mine;*
> *I have built them for you.*
> *Where could such a journey take you*
> *but deeper into Me?*
> *Come! Let us enjoy this walk together."*

Consort

Thinking myself lost,
You have always been leading me
back down into this world transfigured
in You,
and into the grace of my lover's sweet soul
made of Your radiant white light.

Now that my eyes are open
I see that she is Your consort,
and less here for me,
than to reveal You.

By Your grace the root of my soul
has opened to receive her
and instantly
I am dissolved
in the light
of Your ineffable presence.

Yes,
I know.
You are the only One who can return her love;
she is wholly Yours.

If it be Your will,
devour my days
in revealing Your love for her through me
and – perhaps –
I might learn something
of how to love as You do,
even in this passing dream-world.

Clay House

Before the Beloved rescued me from my arrogant
and perfect ignorance,
I thought I knew how to love the beloved
before me.

Now,
in honor of That One,
I will knock on the edge of your clay house
only when moved by Love
to breathe the caress of grace
toward you.

Whether fingertips, lips,
or tongue,
my touch will be a gesture of devotion
to the One whom I know you love
more than me,
an offering to bathe you
with the shimmering presence
of the Friend
you know so intimately.

Peek-a-Boo

It does not speak
yet from it do all true words
come.

It does not move
yet all Creation dances in its dynamic
power.

It does not bend low
yet all things rest upon its
foundation.

Be watchful!
It playfully reveals itself in a moment's
loving gesture.

There!
Did you see it as I came close to kiss
your cheek?

It is the Beloved beyond name and form
Who alone is this Love
that could move me to do so!

Carried Away

Gently comes her touch,
here in this still, dark night;

I stir.

Feather-like fingertips at the center
of my chest,
and instantly my breath deepens
into her peace.

There...
soft, golden light
flowing like satin rivulets through me,
opening my soul to its roots deep
in the Beloved.

Together we celebrate at the altar of our union.

There is a sound emerging uncreated,
and now the stream of golden wine
carries us away,
away to the Breath within the breath
and the One within the two.

Carried away, carried away.

Upside Down

The emptier I become
the fuller I am.

The more I confess my ignorance before
the utter mystery of Love
does Love come to wrap me in Her
sweet revelations.

How little I know,
how unaccomplished I am!

Look not to me,
for I have nothing.

All I can offer
is what has been given me by grace:
recognition of your perfect innocence,
a gentle touch of peace,
and a whispered reminder that you are
and have always been
wholly G-d's.

Two Hearts

Wherever two hearts have surrendered
beyond the dream of the dreamer
it becomes clear that only Love
is real.

Fear of loss is unimaginable
and the thought of possessing one another
is but a comedy,
good only for a moment's
belly laugh.

Our Journey

Here is our journey.

While we sleepwalk
our suffering bounces us
from relationship to relationship
and we utter each time:
"I have never known a love like this!"

As grace awakens us
and we taste
the limited freedom of directing
the desire of love – choosing more judiciously -
we utter:
"I have never known a love like this!"

Finally,
surrendered in G-d
one mantra is chanted without ceasing – there -
in the silence beneath our minds, whether alone or not:
"I have never known a love like this!"

Reclined at last in the Beloved One,
the gift of holy relationships arises effortlessly
from the soil of our ceaseless praise
of The Shimmering One
and together (at last) we sing:
"We have never known a Love like this!"

Want love?
Let your life become an act of ceaseless praise.

The Best of Sex

May we all discover
that the only way to love is to
cease insisting on control of
our lovers.

Let us all be shaken from the grip of the Imposter
by our unbridled passion
as Love seeps finally
into this
frenzied and sickened world
of fear.

In this way,
we may get some idea
of how the Beloved longs to love us.

You see,
the only way to know That One
is to love as That One first
loves us.

Control and calculation get only a grade of 'C',
while Appreciation, Acceptance and Allowance
get 'A's!

Someday it will be this way for everyone, you know.

And Heaven will have landed upon
this earth.

Soul

All We Need to Remember

The Reed Flute

The music of the reed flute
attracts the soul
because it has arisen from mud and water
to become bamboo,
a perfect gift for playing love songs
devoted to the Beloved.

Arouse the shining soul within you
from its long, long sleep
and begin sounding the sweet notes
of Love's perfect peace!

Second Birth

Every soul is on a journey.
Until we realize the fullness
of the Self within the self,
expressing the deepest compassion,
forgiveness, service, and creativity
waiting to pour through our hearts to coat this world,
Life has not begun.

For enlightenment is the artistic process
of G-d's journey *into* the soul,
and not the other way 'round.

The Beloved melts resistances
and pounds away at the stones of our
well-defended positions,
knowing like water flowing to the sea:
rocks don't stand a chance.

Worn smooth
we become welcomed stepping-stones
for the Beloved's children
as they pass from this moment to the next,
and always in Her.

Finally,
we are mystic lovers whose lives reveal
the roots of the Soul beyond our own souls.
Every sage is humbled to discover that the end sought
is but the true beginning of Life,
and all that went before mere shadow-dreams.

Many existences may pass
before the soul awakens and makes of itself a gift
on the altar of the Beloved,
wrapped in papers of gratitude and ribbons of humility.

Then begins the alchemy of the
Second Birth.

Not a single soul has ever found an escape from this.

Oops!

For years I toiled away in the Imposter's basement
thinking that cleaning, rearranging and even remodeling
was a good use of time.

Little did I know what a good and cheap employee I was.

For everything I called "me" and "mine"
was the property of the Imposter,
and only that usurper gained from my efforts
to be more, have more, know more, do more.

Now I see,
and you will, too,
if you are willing to follow this pathless path
revealing no stepping stone
until you decide to step forward in faith.

When the Imposter's grip is finally vanquished,
keep nothing for your self.
Give the spoils to G-d,
and let the soul become its true being:
a servant to,
and sacred lover of,
the Beloved One.

And no matter what,
never threaten a strike because you don't like the wages!
Quick as a wink,
you will only accomplish casting yourself yet again
from this cosmic Union.

The Friend

Grace Takes a Shape
to Which We May Respond

The Friend

The Friend
Who waits to reveal the Way
is always here.

Passing through the doorway
of your willing heart,
She will not remain
hidden.

A Question for the Avatar

Venus has revealed herself before me,
here, as you.

Sophia has revealed herself before me,
here, as you.

Aphrodite has revealed herself before me,
here, as you.

Oh, Friend,
what grace has brought me here
to stand with you in the threshold between the two worlds:
one made by the One you Love,
and one made by the rest of us still in love
with ourselves?

Now,
it is over for me.
What choice do I have but to learn
how to empty the bottle of this body and mind
to receive you,
and take off the cap so you can pour yourself
out into the world?

By the way...

How did you get all that Feminine Light
into the space and volume of a male body
those many years ago?

The High Mountain

Once I climbed a high mountain
to meet the Friend.

I asked him how he lives.

This was His reply:

> *"I rest in peace,*
> *having released all shadows.*
>
> *I abide in Joy,*
> *desiring nothing save to extend*
> *this Light of the Beloved which has revealed*
> *all things to me.*
>
> *Knowing not where I go,*
> *judging not where I have been,*
> *I rest in the eternal presence of G-d,*
> *and trust alone That One from Whom*
> *I have emerged.*
>
> *The Beloved speaks.*
>
> *I listen.*
>
> *Claiming nothing but ignorance,*
> *I live as a dance of flowing waters, here,*
> *beyond all space and time,*
> *ceaselessly muttering beneath my breath,*
> *'Ah, this blessed Journey!'*
>
> *Here, I wait, for someone like you."*

Oh, Friend!
(In praise of Jeshua ben Joseph)

Oh friend,
you have shown me the way
to the Castle!

I could not accept you on faith,
like so many others.

I could not accept you through religion,
like so many others.

You,
born from so much Love,
found a way to emerge in shimmering light
inside this fortress I had made to keep safe distance
from the love that transforms.

You have taken everything,
seducing me in Love to empty my baskets
until I saw: Abba is here!

Now I am dissolved in Him,
like you.
Wandering in Eden,
with you.

Oh friend,
there is none like you!
Seducer of the false self, master of all Creation,
you who ceaselessly longs
to give away the Christ mind you found
in the castle of the King.

I am forever humbled
at the sight of your splendor,
and I prostrate myself before your wisdom.

Oh, way-shower!
In you am I undone,
and only G-d's breath breathes this self
made from dust.

I dip my cup without ceasing
in the well that rests here,
in the silent center of the King's chamber,
offering it to passersby.

But I am only a beginner.
I cannot hold a candle to you!

If ever I succeed
in giving away to this world
some tiny fraction of the cascading ocean of grace
you have placed me under,
I might taste a moment of fulfillment
in revealing to you this gratitude
that overwhelms my soul.

Gifts of Sophia
Fruits from Well Planted Seeds

A Piece of Coal

Once upon a time
a miner pulled up a piece of coal
and began applying the pressure necessary
to turn the coal into a diamond.

But all the coal could do
was wail and lament
its separation from its past
deep in the earth, asleep.

So persistent was it that the miner put it back
and continued on his way,
searching for another prime piece.

After all,
he owns the mine
and will be this way again,
next year, or the next...

Such a shame!
The piece of coal could have enjoyed
its transfiguration into a reflector of light
and even shortened the time
from Nothing to Something.

Embrace this crushing pressure
applied by One Who knows more
than any piece of coal could hope to
even on its best of days,
and let the Beloved squeeze out of you
everything obstructing the diamond your soul can be.

The Presence That Doesn't

Who can say from where this has all arisen?
The scientists are ignorant,
the priests only pretend to know
and the highest sages
are reticent in the end to say anything at all.

Can we discover a single thing
that knows neither beginning nor end?

Oh, yes.

This majestic Presence which is *here*,
pervading all things while free of all things,
carrying us all on its wings,
carrying us away to what we will be.

Finding this Presence
turns seekers into finders
and doers into servants
of the Ever-Shimmering One.

Finding this Presence
is what a cloud feels when it disappears
into the clear and empty sky,
reappearing as a rainbow arching over two lovers
entwined in a meadow
of buttercups.

Karma to Dharma

Aha!
The joke's on me!
Your wondrous beauty was too much to resist,
and so I pursued you,
fueled by obsession born of the times
you let me kiss your neck.

Too late,
I learned the power of possessing You
for my own pleasure
was the last vestige to be purged
before I could lie with You in the marriage-bed
of creature and Creator.

There can be no freedom *for* the self,
only *from* it.

Is there a choice but to this purging?
To think so
is the very spell of the Imposter.

Here is the secret:

From the moment we were birthed into existence
the Beloved has been fashioning us
into the Mystical Christ
not for our good,
but Hers!

As a stream flows inexorably to the sea,
our karma wrapped in acceptance and love
carries us to our dharma.

Like A Jewel

This wave arising just now:
from where has it come?

It brings the sound of deep silence
after its tumultuous apex crashes and dies,
depositing it here like a jewel before a King.

Ceaselessly Her ocean knocks on the inner door,
but not everyone who walks these shores
hears the soundless sound these waves bring
from the deep well of the Beloved.

Not everyone opens
beyond the edge of the Imposter's world
and so miss the gift of Love offered them
through their lovers,
but from the Ever-Shimmering One,
receiving only what they have chosen to see there:
the veil that separates the soul from the Soul.

Look beyond
what you think you want,
and discover
what you have always needed.

The Joke is on Me

I can only laugh and shake my head:
I've been tricked, seduced!

Everyone who lives here in this Garden says the same.

This world is mere appearance and trickery
and all my seriousness
the cause of the angels' entertainment.

In dying beyond the root of my self
I saw the face of my Beloved
and even this body seemed suddenly a fraud.

What else could I do with this useless baggage
but give it to Her to do with as she pleases,
knowing the purpose and meaning I had given it
was never more
than a silly delusion and whim?

On a good day,
perhaps I will hear my Beloved
reveal the Truth that sets another free
through this strange collection of molecules.

I can no longer imagine it being good for anything else.

Mask-Maker

I came into this world just like everyone else.

The world said to me:
"You can't be here without a mask."

Naively believing a sea of mask-wearers,
I set about to make my own.
I am afraid I became so engrossed
that I did little else for nearly thirty years.

At least I was never alone.

I grew weary.

My masks could not caress me,
nor let in the precious pulsing of Life.

Born in me was an insatiable longing for the scent
of my Beloved,
for the ecstasy of being swallowed whole
in Her radiance.

I looked for Her everywhere.

When it all seemed futile and I was exhausted
Grace gave me my desire, but I wanted Her no longer!
I only wanted to die in Her,
to serve Her,
to be carried away to my ruin in Her.

Then,
the eyes of my heart opened,
truly opened:

My Beloved was everywhere!

The self is the entrance fee
for this secret and constant orgasm only
the enlightened can see.

The One Request

From the moment I gave up being right
and stopped defending my perceptions
in favor of owning my own ignorance,
my Beloved has swept me up
in Her arms.

That One has been carrying me ever since
into ever-expanding realms
of Her precious and infinite pure Being.

Her only request is this:
That I unceasingly surrender the space
in my soul
once all plugged up with thoughts of "I" and "mine"
that she might rule my tiny kingdom
of existence.

She makes this request of everyone.
Don't waste yet more time negotiating!

The Gambler

Most people want in their religion
what they want in their investments:
a sure winner.

At least,
they want someone else to minimize their risk!

The Beloved is never revealed in this way
for She find worthiness only in those
willing to gamble themselves away
for Love.

To them does she come
as they sleepwalk through this dream world.

If you want safety,
invest with caution.

If you want G-d,
abandon caution,
and dare to love
as the Beloved loves.

"And how is that?" you ask.

The answer cannot be spoken.

Only discovered and lived.

Mystic Fool

Seekers are constantly involved
in all manner of ritual and debate,
ever hoping to catch a glimpse of the Beloved.

But the mystic who has been ravaged by Her
simply embraces each moment
and is devoured anew by Her
over and over eternally.

Having thrown away the Imposter,
there is no more striving, no more seeking.

Here, the fruit has ripened: the Lover in us awakens.

Reject nothing!
Allow this transient existence
to be transformed
through your unobstructed feeling-embrace.
Ask only to be devoured by the Beloved
and She is immediately revealed.

But we have secretly wanted *anything* but Her,
and so have stored up sad dramas
or clung to the false hope of security for tomorrow.

How will we find G-d
if we do not submit to loving
as She loves?

Hear now this:
Love does not condemn.

Resisting this no longer,
the Imposter slips gently into enlightenment
as a dewdrop slips into the ocean.

Arise, mad lover.

This Old House

The house we have all purchased jointly,
gathering a sea of trinkets to fill every empty corner,
is not our Home.

The Craftsman did not build it;
only the Imposter wearing sheep's clothing
while we unwittingly signed our life away
to the beguiling appearance
within us.

Strike the flame of only a little willingness
and watch it reduced to ashes!

Don't worry.
This is what the Craftsman has been
waiting for.

Let's be homeless together awhile,
freed of all those useless trinkets,
left with nothing but infinity
shining at us through each other's eyes.

Let's give the Craftsman time to build us a palace,
here in the soft grasses of the heart's
sacred intimacy.

Mocking the Beloved

If I say I love G-d,
but require another to be my possession,
I am a foolish hypocrite.

If I say I love G-d,
but am ashamed of this body and its passions,
or yours,
I spew forth mockery on the Beloved Creator
who creates to extend Herself
for joy.

Better for all if
That One
devour me in its fire
as a mistake quickly
forgotten.

May Lightening Strike

Who sits in the safe confines of their cellar
while the lightning storm rages
misses the surge of power, the ecstatic brilliant flashes
illuminating distant hills
invisible in the normal haze of the day.

Run to your rooftops
and stand on the edge of the precipice
fearing a fall into darkness;
transformation only occurs at the edge.

This is what it means to risk the heart for Love.

Our illusions remain hidden
when we rest in our comfort zones
built 'round our hearts
thinking to keep the Imposter safe.

It is there,
in the alchemical fires of risking
everything for Love -
under the influence of perfect vulnerability -
that the supernal Lightening strikes,
revealing what has been held back
from the embrace of
the Beloved.

Leave your cellars!

Fruit on the Tree

Have you ever noticed that trees which soar skyward
looking all grand and powerful
bear no fruit?

But trees which bear good fruit
bend toward the earth.

So, too,
the mystic lover
who would be devoured by the Beloved
and know the Great Secret of freedom
does not reach for heights,
but plumbs the depths of the soul,
no matter how lowly or foul time so spent
might seem to those aspiring to be seen
as majestic trees.

Disappearing

Dawn blew gently 'cross my face
until I left my slumber
and gave myself like a puppy on a leash
to some unseen master on an unknown mission.

Pulled to this deserted beach
I sit transfixed by the immense full moon
sitting on the ocean's horizon
like a voluptuous woman on the lap of humanity.

She changed her brilliant colors
as the first rays of the day grew over the crest
of the eastern mountain
to kiss her into passionate shades of blush.

Suddenly,
the moon vanished!

It was no match for the rising sun.

Then I knew
why the Friend had called me here
from my slumber.

Our illusions are like the moon,
so tempting and large and familiar.

But our love?

Our love is like the sun.

No One Here

Guess what!
It is not Love we are seeking
but its expression which compels the soul.

All that we do is some attempt
to fulfill what we are created for:
extending into the visible the invisible Reality
of the Beloved.

As we turn 'round to caress
the shadowy echoes of useless fears
our doing is expressed more and more lovingly,
which means there is less of "me" doing the doing!

Finally,
in a quiet moment of consummate death
that no one but the Beloved notices,
only Love arrives to do the doing.

Such a life is incomprehensible,
unfathomable, and utterly unacceptable
to those who worship at the altar
of the Imposter.

If you need anyone to notice
you have awakened into Life
you have not yet died into
the Beloved.

Sleeping Stones

Once in a former life
I was a small pebble resting in the dirt
at the edge of flowing lava.

You were there too.

At times,
we were parched from the summer sun.

At others,
drenched in winter rains.

Constantly the Friend whispered to us:

> *"Fall into the flowing lava and become the fire*
> *that turns the ocean to steam,*
> *releasing it back into Me."*

But we were too busy shouting back and forth, "Hold on!"

At least we knew how to endure being sun-baked
or drenched in a quagmire.

Sleeping stones think this is reasonable,
but we were simply too afraid
of the Fire that turns stones into
fine gold.

Do you remember?
When fear ruled our kingdoms
and we believed our shared dream of being
mere bodies in space?
This is the reason for the Friend's appearance;
the proof of Grace.

Now we laugh.
Now we are here in the Beloved's garden,
playing together,
needing nothing but to love one another
simply for the fun of it.

That's what Spirit does.

But of course, you know that.

The Caravan

Oh, beloved sojourners,
let us not fear our fears, judge our sadness,
nor chastise each our tears.

What would happen in this world
if we befriended the demon of our loneliness
and walked hand in hand openly enjoying
our Ignorance and Confusion
about our existence,
instead of pretending otherwise?

No tree reaches the sky
unless its roots penetrate deep into the earth.

There,
in the unseen darkness
and unnoticed by the world of pretenders,
the elixir is discovered that bursts the branches
toward the sun.

What good does it do to keep up the ruse
that all is well?

That is like living in an empty beer can
chanting the mantra:

"At least we know this place."

There is a Great Mystery,
a caravan of gold and jewels and frankincense and myrrh
waiting patiently for us...

Waiting for us to enter through the Door
beyond this feeble world
of plastic smiles and numbing idols.

Waiting beyond this sad tale of *me* and *mine*
there in the oasis we all secretly seek
near the pool of *We, our G-d's*.

Just a peek through this Door will blind us
to the value once given the valueless
and we will wonder in awe:

"Who's caravan might this be?"

There is a Place

There is a place flesh cannot touch
and even the breath must be silent
at this altar.

Nowhere a place for the Imposter to gain entrance.

The Beloved Herself dwells here
as the Self of every "I";
the source of every loving gesture
occasionally breaking through us into this world.

Everyone owns the pink slip of this domain
but, sadly,
very few ever bother to build their homes here.

Instead,
they settle for an occasional visit,
often passing through
by accident.

They spend most of their time
swimming in maya's ocean
chanting the mantra of all suffering:
"What about me?"

Become That Fire

What fire is this
that consumes no wood
and is unlit by my own matches?

Who placed it in this hearth
'round which my soul came into existence?

Knowing neither beginning nor end,
it is the Beloved's very Breath.

This fire is not of my making,
and so what is most truly *me*
is not *mine* at all!

Since the taproot is not mine,
perhaps I should give back to That One
all the branches of *me* I had imagined to be *mine*.

Only a fool addicted to cheap wine
would keep up the Imposter's exhaustive resistance
to what is inevitable.

Go ahead.
Die into that fire.

Become the Living Word.

In G-d's Defense

The only way out is through.
Grace is not what saves us from the Imposter's effects.
It is that which transforms them into the stepping-stones
to the King's mansion.

We must eventually live that which heals our karma:
choosing for Love in lessons revisited one final time,
for Love – the real kind – ends time.

Insight, no matter how illumined, is never sufficient.
For only what is embodied is known,
and G-d is forever realized
by living forever deeper into G-d.

To be awake means only that we know this
and are gladly surrendered to this Pathway;
free not because some end is attained,
but because there is no more delusion called:
"this is *my* life!"

There is no limit in G-d.
And so let us embrace the sobering truth
that we will never be *finished*.

Since this is so,
what good is it to care about being right?
Or even arguing that we can be?

Can the unfinished ever hope to prove
they know anything at all?

There is no final completion.

Sobering, isn't it?

Let us live in wonder, abide in forgiveness, and see only innocence.

Just love the Beloved.

Where Goodness Shines

Where goodness shines all hearts are healed.
Where tears flow in gratitude peace is restored.

There are some who walk this world
with the wisdom of the bird who sings before the dawn
is birthed from the night.

They alone are bearers to us all
of the Light
drawn down from the heart
of the Beloved.

They light the lanterns of our souls
with the delight of certainty,
igniting our embrace of all that yet waits within us
to pour out as sweet blessings upon this world.

In their presence we are awakened
from the slumber of our doubt
and quickened with the pulse of Joy
that restores the soul to its created brilliance.

For them do I offer these words,
written with knees touching the ground
and head gently bowed before my simple altar.
We all know of them,
these angels of the Shimmering One
who have come to kiss us here
in the heart of our hearts.

They bring back to us the memory of heaven,
revealing the only real purpose this world can ever have.

G-d bless you, sweet angels.

Become Wise

Man created glass
to let the light of the sun touch him
as he rests in his cave,
safely tucked away from the savage elements.

Become wise.
Learn what brings the Beloved's light
near to you.
Don't venture out to find it!

Create in the temple of your body
a sepulcher in which to rest
from the Imposter's incessant droning
that you might be missing something out there.

Silence, dear pilgrim,
is a light magnet.

Drink deep. Let wisdom blossom.

Purest Gold

The great dream
is trying to convince ourselves
that we are counterfeit coins.

But we are molded from Love's infinite storehouse
of pure and radiant golden light.

See the wealth our position brings us!
Earth and sky and the fragrance of spring grasses;
the intoxicating scent of our lover's sweet passion;
the caress of quiet breathing.

May we all breathe well,
O golden ones,
and share our coins with everyone,
lest that One breathe us back into Itself
as a mistake quickly forgotten!

Intoxicating Embrace

This ceaselessly changing dance
of light and shadow
offers no hope of peace!

Unless we release our resistance to it
and ask nothing from it,
becoming only a conduit
through which the Beloved delights
in the intoxicating embrace of
Her creations.

So let me hug you!

The Fisherman

The old man stood at the ocean's edge
not more than fifty yards from the tourists
on their lounge chairs
waiting to be nudged by the bearer of yet another drink.

The old man cast his net.
Seeing it was empty, he simply cast it again.

Who can receive miracles
save those who follow the fisherman's example?

Heaven is closer than this ocean lapping at his feet.
Knowing this, he does not leave.

Come!
Cast your net into the Beloved's ocean.

At least spend as much time in this way
as a tourist spends by the pool.

Get drunk on this golden elixir!

Performance Anxiety

Stillness is the threshold to the Beloved's bed chamber.

Why would you linger
in the worlds of your busyness
when the One you really want is waiting there,
warmed by divine love-wine,
and wanting you so badly?

Let us hope it is not the illusion of performance anxiety!

The door is unlocked. Cross the threshold.

The Shimmering One
will orchestrate your love-making
while never ceasing to whisper into your ear:

> *"You need do nothing but receive Me."*

Silver Palms

Unable to sleep
I went and stood beneath the full moon
and saw that even these palm trees
had been turned to silver.

So entranced was I
that I lost sight of my Beloved,
forever shining beyond all form.

A moment of forgetting is human, I suppose.

But this world is only a pale reflection
of that glorious Light
and no moon can ever hope to reveal it fully.

Don't waste a lifetime gathering silver
when the goldsmith is so near,
resting and waiting in your own silent center.

Go ahead right now.

Turn away from this silvery world
like a tortoise withdrawing its limbs inward
and wait for the Beloved's supernal Light
to show you what alone has
real value.

I See You

Don't you think I can see
that the restlessness in your soul
is due to your secret yearning
to know the Shimmering One?

The memory of dancing in G-d
has been quickened to life again by a droplet of grace;
by yourself,
you are incapable of the desire for G-d.

Now,
in each of your moments
your soul is being woven in glimmering golden threads
by the cosmic weaver Herself!

Her only intent is to make your soul into the magic carpet
that will fly you away from this world
of dream-shadows,
into this ever-deepening gift of
Her Presence.

Call me when you arrive. We'll do lunch!

The Tortoise and the Hare

I know you.
You want the short course
and the speed of the hare
to reach the Beloved's banquet
all the mystics are raving about.

Leave the long, slow course to all those cautious tortoises.

Very well, then!

This *avadhoota* (crazy adept)
will break the sacred seal and tell you
the well-kept Secret:

All you need do is realize a life
in which all things – *all things* –
are known as perfect Grace;
scented petals falling from the Beloved's rose garden,
sent only to reveal Her sweet, intoxicating Presence.

Have you tasted it yet?
It devours all that arises and passes away by loving it,
to death.

Just rest here without ceasing,
and the hare and tortoise are one.

Which Floor?

The body is moved
by the need to survive.

The mind is moved
by the need for personal meaning.

The soul is moved only
by the need for the kiss of G-d,
even if it does not yet know this.

Recline, then,
away from body and mind,
resting the soul as close to those lips as possible.

Then, closer still, again and again.

Be ravaged by them
until survival and meaning are forgotten
like toys outgrown.

Be swept away in this great Love.

Who Arrives?

And so it came to pass
that the pilgrim had heard enough convincing words
about the abode of the Beloved.

She sat with the old wise one, who said:

"So, you are off to find the Ever-Shimmering One?"

"Yes!" replied the student.

"Just remember," the old wise one replied,
"the one who ends the Journey will not be
the one who begins it."

This is why no one can know G-d.

Let's hope this pilgrim goes beyond
the priests and soothsayers sprouting up by the dozen
in this ever-shallower world of ours,
and consents to being re-made into one who is known
by G-d.

For G-d knows only what she alone fashions
from unshaped clay into fine porcelain.

Be cut and carved, and fear not the Fire.

Now…

Take a deep breath…

Open your mouth, and let the exhale
go with a sigh.

Then, take several more breaths,
allowing the body to stretch.

. . . . .

No souls come together in any context
by accident.

By grace, we have found ourselves joined
through this little book, placed here by G-d
through our willingness to join.

And to join is to heal.

May all beings come to join us,
reclined in the True Soul of our souls.

Thank you, G-d, for our life.
Our life IS your Life.
Thank you, thank you, thank you.

Jayem

About the Author

Jayem is often referred to as 'a Teacher of teachers'—a rare blend of enlightenment coupled with a true mastery of both teaching and facilitation of healing and forgiveness.

Following his return from Vietnam, he delved deeply into the practices of meditation and yoga, and much of the years 1973–87 were spent teaching them, while also receiving academic degrees in comparative religion, philosophy, and psychology. His own journey took him deeply into emerging body-centered therapies and family-of-origin healing, including birth and womb trauma.

He shares that he has lived in three questions passionately, with each 'living him into' their answers; each is a progressive stage of Enlightenment:

Who am I, and what is all this?

How might I heal into real Enlightenment, and then serve others in doing the same?

And finally,

How can I learn to love as God loves?

From his extraordinary relationship with Jeshua, a large body of Wisdom Teachings has emerged, referred to as the PathWay—from channeled audios of Jeshua to books, online courses, videos, and retreats and pilgrimages to sacred places held all over the world, along with his inspiring On-Line Ashram program.

To find out more please visit ***www.wayofmastery.com*** or Jayem's Facebook page at ***www.facebook.com/wayofmastery***

The Way of Mastery PathWay

The PathWay offers a comprehensive roadmap if you have the desire to **grow, heal** and **know** yourself truly.

It includes **five core texts, additional materials** and a series of alchemical **living practices** which offer support that ideas alone cannot achieve.

The Five Core Texts

1 ~ *The Jeshua Letters*
2 ~ *The Way of the Heart*★
3 ~ *The Way of Transformation*★
4 ~ *The Way of Knowing*★
5 ~ *The Way of the Servant*

★Also available as the original audio.

Living Practices ~ additional material

LovesBreath, Radical Enquiry, the unveiled original teachings of *The Aramaic Lord's Prayer* and *The Aramaic Beatitudes,* meditations including the much-loved *In the Name,* together with the in-depth darshans of the Online Ashram—these are all key elements of the PathWay.

Living Practices ~ insight groups, workshops, retreats and pilgrimages

From small informal groups to our global pilgrimages, Friends of the Heart gather to grow together.

You can find out more about the PathWay and all that it offers by visiting our website, where a wealth of video and audio excerpts, and much more, awaits you:

www.wayofmastery.com

www.ingramcontent.com/pod-product-compliance
Lightning Source LLC
LaVergne TN
LVHW011423080426
835512LV00005B/241